My Rules:

How to Create and Support a Respectful Leadership Culture

By Bob Short

Bob Short MA

How to Create and Support a Respectful Leadership Culture

A Collection of Rules by
Bob Short

Copyright @ 2026 Bob Short

ISBN: 978-1-62249-763-8

Published by

Biblio Publishing

Columbus, Ohio

BiblioPublishing.com

Dedication

This book is dedicated to all the individuals who have provided support to me during my 40 plus years of working in the mental health care system. This includes my family, especially my wife Diana for her continuous faith in my ability to lead others successfully. My coworkers who worked together with me and celebrated so many accomplishments that we now find ourselves as closest friends. Together we have faced the multiple challenges related to the demanding work of providing care to individuals who are in the most need of support and care.

"Learn Something.

Apply It.

Pass it on so

it is not Forgotten."

Rush Asawa

My Rules: How to Create and Support a Respectful Leadership Culture

Chapter 1: Rules for Supervisors / Successful Managers
Tell People What You Want Them to Do

Staff Don't Want to Mess Up

Don't Bring a Problem Forward Without Bringing a Solution

Don't Negotiate with Terrorists

Chapter 2: Rules for Leaders / Successful Leadership
Get to the "yes"

Use Your Vision to Provide Leadership and Develop Leaders

Define Success and Share It

Use Key Performance Indicators to Standardize Practice

Data Doesn't Lie

Lead with the Right Temperament

Chapter 3: Rules for Management / Successful Change Management
Connect to the Why

Creating an All in Culture

Embrace and Become Comfortable with Adversity

Keep Progress Moving / Don't Quit

Chapter 4: Rules for Promoting Respect
Develop Relationships with Your Friends and Enemies

Feeling Safe is a Must

Become Coercion Free

Promote a Strong Peer Support Program

Forward

I want to lead this publication with what I hold as my core principles. I strongly believe that every person who I have encountered, including the most difficult patient, the most unmanageable staff person, and the most hardnosed manager, has inherent worth and deserve respect.

Through my many years of working in the state psychiatric hospital system of Ohio, I had the opportunity to learn and pass on to my leadership staff significant life lessons. Most of these were related to managing a system that involved the people who work in it, the patients who were treated there, and everything related to the treatment of those people who received care in the system. These lessons I eventually named rules, and during my supervision time with my leadership team, I would reference them often.

In the pages that follow, I share my list of "rules." I organized them around specific topics that leaders, who I have worked with over the years, are challenged with at times. My main message as the title of this book is called "How to Create and Support a Respectful Leadership Culture." The topics include Rules for Supervisors, Rules for Leaders, Rules for Management, and Rules for Promoting Respect. I dedicate this list of rules to all those managers and leaders in health care, especially in a heavily structured environment like a state system where change and creating a rewarding respectful culture is a challenge.

And so, I share with you my leadership rules that I hope demonstrate and support my beliefs as a leader over time ....

How did I get here?

I started my leadership career in the field of mental health services directly out of college, and my first exposure came at Fort Logan Mental Health Center in Denver, Colorado, where I did my occupational therapy internship on a geriatric unit and discovered my calling to mental health care. A few months later, I was hired in my first job as an OT at a thirty-bed, inpatient psychiatric unit for acute care patients at St. Elizabeth's Hospital in Dayton, Ohio, leading therapy groups with a very diverse patient population. I worked there for one year before following my future wife to Columbus, Ohio. Once there, I worked as a case manager at St. Anne's Hospital on second shift of a very acute inpatient psych unit where I was able to add new skills to my behavioral health toolbox.

When I turned 25 years old, I figured it was time to take some risks and began working at the Central Ohio Psychiatric Hospital (COPH), a state operated facility in Columbus. I was hired as a supervisor of an Activity Therapy (AT) program for a brand-new 208 bed geriatric facility, the Kosar Center. As the supervisor of the AT program, I began to learn how to lead my staff of 16, very young music, art, and recreational therapists who had minimal experience in psych or geriatrics. It soon became a time for all of us to learn together.

My short-term plan when I started my tenure at COPH was to work up to two years there before I moved on to something else. Well, that didn't happen for a lot of reasons. First, I got married, and then, I was the recipient of a series of promotions over the next ten years. I became the Director of AT for the whole hospital, including the 700 bed Adult and Geriatric Program. I was eventually named Director of Psychiatric Rehabilitation and developed a program that changed the clinical philosophy of treatment there from institutional care to what is now embraced as recovery-based care. This new emphasis on supporting our patient's ability to live in the community and build on their individual strengths led to the eventual discharging of approximately 300 long-term patients over three years from the hospital.

Major changes began to occur in the hospital's environment during the 1980's based on some significant leadership reorganizing in the state department of mental health. This brought with it a host of managerial challenges. A new funding strategy for community programs led to a decrease in the population of the state hospital system, along with inpatient population downsizing, state hospital closures, and significant state hospital staff reductions.

At that time, I entered the public administration master's degree program at The Ohio State University. After receiving my degree, I decided to move out of my clinical leadership roles to take on more administrative tasks. I eventually was appointed the Chief Operating Officer (COO) of COPH, where I managed hospital resources, budgets, physical plant operations, capital projects, information technology, and human resources. I also coordinated the merger of COPH with a similar state hospital in Dayton that became Twin Valley Behavior Healthcare (TVBH).

Obviously, I again had a lot to learn during my COO work, but throughout my time in these new roles I tried to never forget my clinical roots, especially that supporting the best patient care possible should be my first priority.

Even though I never pursued it as a goal, I became the Chief Executive Officer of TVBH in 2008. It was during this time that I discovered what kind of leader I wanted to be as I implemented strong clinical driven programs, as well as safer and more therapeutic patient unit milieus, that eventually led to the development of the highly successful Respect Initiative program in the hospital. This vision of creating a respectful organization that focused on safety while supporting recovery and trauma informed care became the pillars of how patient treatment was focused in the hospital. Our leadership team eventually shared our program of patient restraint and staff injury reductions as "Best Practices: Safety Guidelines for Injury Free Management of Psychiatric Inpatients in Pre-Crisis and Crisis Situations" which was published in the December 2008 edition of *Psychiatric Services*.

Change followed again when, a few years later, I was appointed the Deputy Director of Hospital Services overseeing the management of all six state hospitals for the Ohio Department of Mental Health, a total operation consisting of 1,000 patients and 2,000 employees. My challenge was to lead and move a system that still viewed itself as six independent hospitals into one that could grow together and embrace best practices. With the help my leadership team, I instituted a new program, The Ohio Hospital System of Care, that met all national standards, as defined by Joint Commission and CMS, and became the new priorities of the state hospitals during this time.

Due to some impending rule changes in the Ohio Public Employee Retirement System, I chose to leave state service and retire in 2012. This was a short-lived break as 90 days later I was asked by Tracy Plouck, the Director of Mental Health, to return to the system part-time and oversee special projects. These ranged from addressing a major reimbursement problem, providing a review of the Information Technology Department, explore the possible implementation of a new electronic health record system, EPIC, and then participating in the design and construction of a new, 208-bed state hospital on the grounds of the same site that I once led as CEO in Columbus. It was a very busy time for me that eventually became full-time, and I was appointed Chief of Hospital Services in 2018, supporting the managers of the state hospital system for the Department of Mental Health and Addictions Services under the leadership of Governor DeWine and Director Lori Criss.

Finally, I believe my biggest challenge besides supporting the implementation of the new EHR and opening a new hospital came during the pandemic when Director Criss appointed me to lead the

COVID vaccination program for the hospital system that eventually provided more than 5,000 doses of vaccine to the staff and patients in the hospitals.

I respectfully retired for the second and last time from the department in December of 2024, having worked for over 45 years leading the hospital system and achieving many of my professional goals, including some I didn't know existed when I began to work there as a young man.

Chapter 1: Rules for Supervisors / Successful Managers

Rule # 1 - Tell people what you want them to do

"Tell people what you want them to do because if you don't, they will make it up and it probably is not what you want them to do".

During my days as a supervisor, manager, director, and leader of an organization, I always made it a practice to meet with the staff that reported to me regularly. Some, I would meet with monthly, others biweekly, or a few weekly if I felt it was necessary. It was during those touch-base meetings that we would review their work projects, staff management issues, and our established goals. Regardless of the frequency of those touch-base meetings, we would always conclude by returning to the subject of what their job was just to stay grounded.

Over the years, many of the leaders that I worked with who were responsible for managing employees complained about the poor performance of their staff or the fact that their employees didn't perform the way that was needed to be successful in their job. It was during my touch-base meetings with those leaders that I would frequently refer to Rule #1 by simply asking this: "do you think they understand what their job is?"

I believe it should be obvious to a manager that if an employee is not performing, then there is a problem. Performance should be measured through the observation of behaviors of the employee. If, for example the expectations are that the employee's job is to come to work and support the clinical care provided in the hospital; then this simple statement that describes expectations should be used to frame most of their discussions moving forward.

Therefore, the manager will need to know if the employee is coming to work, or are they being viewed by others as someone who performs their clinical job duties? In addition are they being responsive to the folks they are supporting? And finally, are they behaving in a way that aligns with the organization's goals of providing quality care?

This then reverts back to my questions to the leadership team members. Such as, are your clinical staff completing their assessments timely and comprehensively? Are they communicating with patients' families and aftercare agencies? Are they completing their discharge summaries, so they meet a specific standard as defined by reviewing bodies? If they don't any of the above, then they are not meeting the expectations of their position.

This rule sounds rather simple, but it is sometimes not used by managers enough especially if they are trying to promote a respectful and supportive work environment. When I tell people what I want them to do, it really is more than how I want them to do their job but also how I want them to perform in that job. Leaders must provide clarity related to what their staff see as their role in the organization. This should always include the expectation that they meet with their employees and provide them with support and guidance while also describing what their work product should be, as defined by them and the employee.

In Summary:

- Have regularly scheduled meetings in person with staff
- Share with staff and confirm with them what you see as their job
- Set Expectations in a clear manner
- Provide support and guidance on what success look like
- Review it during your meetings and share how it fits in the goals of the organization.

Rule # 2 – Staff Don't Want to Mess Up

"I don't believe that people get up in the morning and decide they are going to mess up at work that day."

Over the years, I have heard many stories from managers about employees behaving badly. Individuals who are rude to their coworkers or even their supervisors. Who refuse to follow mandatory procedures or fail to perform a process that is an essential part of their job. All of these negative behaviors or actions are possible, but I do not believe most people start off intentionally choosing to make these kinds of unacceptable decisions

It is my experience that most people want to know what their job is (Rule #1) and also what they need to do to accomplish a task that they are responsible for. I believe that most staff start off their workday with an attitude that emphasizes being successful and wanting to be respected and recognized for good performance.

I have found that unacceptable gaps in an employee's performance are not only related to a lack of understanding with regard to what their job is, but also because they did not receive the training necessary to do what was expected. Many times, during my conversations with managers about their "problem staff members," the manager expressed a belief that just talking to or providing information to their staff was sufficient and therefore any poor performance was intentional.

To be successful, leaders need to embrace training and education but also understand that training is not always communicated in a manner that employees can transform into behavior that is expected. For example, employees need to be assessed by managers related to their understanding of the training and additional follow-up may be needed.

Many times, staff fall back on behaviors that they are comfortable with regardless of whether or not it meets the expectations of the organization. A particular staff member may treat their patients like children rather than adults who need to be empowered to actively participate in their recovery. Or an employee may be rude to a patient who uses a term that is offensive to them. Staff may also have difficulty being therapeutic with someone who has a history of behavior they find unacceptable.

If this occurs, then it becomes the responsibility of the leadership of the organization to create a work environment that provides quality training to staff and supports a respectful workplace. But they also need to support a culture where staff understand their performance expectations, their work goals, and how they fit in with the organization's goals.

It has always been my expectation that managers should embrace this rule and show faith in their staff and that the organization should create and support a respectful work culture where employees will not only choose not to mess up but will choose to excel. In addition, managers must promote recognition and provide positive affirmation when employees are meeting the organization's performance goals.

In Summary:

- People want to be successful at their jobs.
- People want to feel respected and recognized for their work performance
- People do not intentionally make unacceptable decisions
- Managers must do more than provide information to employees and expect improvement
- Managers need to build a culture of respect
- If given the opportunity and motivation, people will choose to excel.

Rule #3 - Don't Bring a Problem Forward without Bringing a Solution

"If I am solving my staff's problems for them then I am doing their job and not supporting their growth."

During my early days as a manager, I would meet with the supervisors in the organization who reported to me. During our check-in times and sometimes during unscheduled meetings, they would bring problems forward to me. I would view these discussions as an opportunity to do some teaching and help my staff grow. I found myself challenged by these interactions, and sometimes I couldn't resist instructing the staff person how they should fix it without asking them what they thought they should do. I took great pride in being able to help these staff with their problems.

Eventually, however, I came to realize that I was not supporting my staff. In fact, I was creating a culture where they became dependent on me, and they would not own their problems and use their own critical thinking skills to figure out how to create their own fixes. I struggled with this, and it took a while for me to figure it out myself. It became apparent however, when one of my direct reports continued to constantly unload his problems on me. Although I relished supporting this individual, I realized that I needed to level with him by simply announcing that I was solving his problems for him, and I felt like I was doing his job. When the employee heard this, he was almost shocked at being challenged by my statement because he was very comfortable dropping his problems in my lap. He even shared with me that he thought that was what I wanted him to do. Of course, this led to Rule #3; "don't bring a problem to me without also bringing a solution.

First, I announced the rule to the managers who reported to me and the expectation of how I wanted my staff to communicate problems. It really did not take long before they learned what was expected. Some became uncomfortable with the new process because before they could blame me for a decision that was made. They also had to learn that I didn't always agree with their solution. Many times, they were told to go back and come up with a different solution that I could support. In fact, sometimes I would have to send them away several times before they could come up with what I agreed was a workable solution.

After a while, Rule #3 became a slogan in the organization. The managers became committed to fixing their issues by owning their problems, their solutions, and their successes while leaders became committed to supporting them.

In Summary:

- Staff can solve their own problems
- By defining and owning a problem staff can create solutions
- Coming to their manager with solutions will assist staff in the development of their critical thinking skills

Rule #4 - Don't Negotiate with Terrorists

"Responding to demands by employees should never be rewarded"

I sometimes encountered a staff person who had inflated opinions of themself, especially related to how valuable they were to the organization. In some cases, these individuals went so far as to make excessive demands on their manager or even the highest-level supervisor, such as requesting a raise or even a promotion rather than engage in a conversation that was respectful in nature. No matter how accurate their opinion may have been regarding their importance, it did not give them permission to engage in such disrespectful behavior. I classified these individuals as "terrorists".

My approach here was a simple one. First, I would attempt to identify if performance issues were present. Also, I would consider if this employee clearly was exemplary and a good or very good performer or if they were a troublemaker. Past performance evaluations would be reviewed and assessed on whether promotions or raises would be appropriate. Whether they were exemplary or a difficult employee, I always put together a strategy for them.

If they had demonstrated behavior that supported our mission, I may have looked at ways to reward them for being a good employee. For example, some of those options included allowing the individual to attend valuable training opportunities or giving them additional responsibilities including leadership on a special project. If they did not show to me that they deserved any type of positive response, then my response would have been likewise. The point here is that responding to demands by employees should rarely be rewarded as it will foster more of this type of behavior in an organization.

If a staff person walked into my office and threatened to quit unless given a raise , then the answer is easy. The best and most appropriate response to this behavior should be a standard one. I would pull out a preprinted resignation letter from my desk drawer and offer it to the person on the spot.

The end goal for these types of interactions should never be "my way or the highway," but rather, it should be a conversation that includes a respectful interaction that will lead to a better relationship with you and the employee. If a positive conversation can occur without threats, then the employee will walk away understanding that making demands of the boss is not acceptable and will not be rewarded by the organization.

I would consistently share this scenario with hospital and system leaders because too many times, leaders back down from insisting on respectful conversations with individuals based on a fear that they would lose the employee. I always emphasized to all staff that when we interact with employees who don't value the organization above themselves, then the value of that person is lessened and should not be supported by their managers.

In Summary:

- How you respond to your staff will create issues in your organization if not managed well
- "My way or the highway" and staff threats are unacceptable behaviors
- Respectful interactions as a leader will support a culture that promotes respect
- If you Interact and give in to employees who value themselves above the organization and their fellow staff, then you lessen the value of that person.

Chapter 2: Rules for Leaders / Successful Leadership

Rule #5 – Get to the Yes

"Can you get me to a yes on this?"

The origin of this rule came from a discussion I had several years ago with the Director of the Ohio Department of Mental Health and Addiction Services. Because of my extensive history with the agency, I was often called on to provide background information on how and why the system operated in a certain way. It was during one of those meetings, that the Director challenged me to create a solution to a long-standing problem between our agency and another in the state. I proceeded to explain to her all the reasons why our department had decided not to implement the changes she wanted, and why other directors had preferred not to do what she proposed. She listened very carefully and finally asked me a simple question: "Can you get me to a yes on this?"

This is not an uncommon situation as many times leaders are asked to get something done that they may not support. Therefore, my quandary really boiled down to how I was going to do something for the boss that I had previously been able to successfully resist from happening with several directors over many years.

Now, I had to be my own adversary and create something that would demonstrate that it was possible to do what was being asked while not weakening the department's position in working with the other agency. I decided it was best to define broadly what the "yes" could look like. So, I ended up redefining what needed to be done and created something that met my director's goal without putting the department at risk. This was complicated because I had to get to the "yes" for her even though it was not exactly where she started. It also would require her to accept what a redefined "yes" would look like.

My style in developing plans for high level leadership staff like this began by providing a one-page document or outline that included a brief description of the situation as well as the defined goal or end product. By sharing this with leadership early in the planning process for this project, it allowed me to shape a solution that could be redefined if the audience agreed with where I, as the author, wanted to land on the project. This required a few meetings with the stakeholders of the proposed change so I could close the deal. Therefore, by me owning the document or plan I was able to keep control.

In this situation, I eventually was able to get us to a "yes" by developing a plan that the director agreed would get her and the department to where she wanted it to go related to working with the other agency. I eventually had to compromise on some of my preconceived weaknesses to the concept and the director approved of a somewhat different goal, but the change was made, and the end-product was achieved without me having too much heart burn (secondary goal).

The approach that I used to successfully provide the director with what she wanted was achieved through my ability to communicate with her in way that she felt respected. I was therefore able to get her to a "yes" that no one previously had been able to.

In Summary:

- Define broadly what the "yes" could look like
- Shape a solution that could be redefined by the audience, but manage it yourself
- By communicating respectfully, acceptance of your plan is predictable

Rule #6 – Use Your Vision to Provide Leadership and Develop Leaders

"The best process that I found when I wanted to move an organization or a group of staff toward a specific goal was to use a process that utilized a vision."

How do you become a leader and develop leaders? There have been many books written about this subject, but I would like to simplify this rule by describing a process that I have found that can be successful for anyone seeking to lead any organization.

Sharing a vision of what I wanted staff to support and where I wanted the organization to go has always been my starting point. This first step required me to know where I was going and describe my path to get there. I call this approach "Follow me and come this way."

For example, when I was appointed the new CEO at Twin Valley Behavior Healthcare, I identified "Respect" as a theme for hospital leaders to embrace. The goal was for anyone who entered our building to feel respect. This included an expectation that respectful interactions should occur everywhere, including supervisors to supervisors, supervisors to staff, staff to staff, staff to patients, patients to patients, and patients to staff.

I created a workgroup that included managers, direct line staff from all areas, union leaders, peer supporters and patients. The group was empowered to develop a respect-focused initiative that would be shared and embraced by everyone. I attended the workgroup as a member only but provided support for their ideas. My goal for this group was for them to not just lead the project but also develop "respect leaders" in all the areas of the organization.

Members of the work group hosted small groups in each discipline to discuss the initiative. The agenda of these small groups included a session on defining what respect looks like and how they could demonstrate it in their everyday work. Anyone who attended one of these sessions received a sticker that they could place on their name tag as a symbol that they were now "respect champions." The stickers soon became a novelty, and staff were asking to join a respect session so they could be part of the initiative.

Posters were created and found their way to walls in hallways everywhere. Monthly "respect champion staff" were identified, and they had their picture in the quarterly newsletter. Respect became an ongoing part of the culture of the organization, and employees regardless of their role became "respect" leaders.

Eventually, I began holding leadership meetings with all the different level managers. I encouraged them to seek out leaders in their work areas. I asked them to support those leaders as they become models for everyone to embrace a culture that promoted the goals of the organization. Therefore, as I implemented Rule #6, I simply provided a vision of something that all staff could relate to, and they soon became comfortable with being led and leading others to embrace this new vision.

In Summary:

- Your vision statement should be clear and easy to understand
- Start with goal language that staff can relate to and includes "follow me and come this way"
- Involve and support a team of leaders that will be empowered to get it to the finish line.

Rule #7 – Define Success and Share It

"As leaders, we need to be able to define what success looks like to our organization so our staff can appreciate their efforts and know where they fit as they attempt to achieve success"

After I retired for the first time and returned to the agency to work on special projects, I was asked to lead three different state hospitals in our system as the acting CEO during some needed transitions. Each time I walked into those organizations, I started working with their leadership team and staff from all areas on defining what success should look like for their hospital. The areas that we identified were very basic but certainly something that could be achieved. They included the following: reducing the length of stay (LOS) for patients, minimizing usage of restraints, lowering staff and patient injuries and eliminating mandated nursing overtime.

All of the areas that were identified required plans that would include interventions as well as specific success measures. The plans became "how to" documents related to the areas that needed improvement. The following brief "how to" plans were rolled out to levels of staff in all areas of the hospital so they could participate in the success.

1) Restraint usage was reduced when early clinical interventions were introduced as part of clinical crisis management plans for clinical staff to utilize. For example, staff began to identify patient triggers and comfort plans as well as safety plans. All of these were developed for all patients who had a history of violence.

2) Staff and patient injuries were minimized by eliminating "hands on" interventions when interacting with patients prior to or during a crisis. Utilization of a "Bad News Protocol" became standard and was implemented by all clinical staff when they became aware of situations where patients received negative responses to questions by anyone.

3) Average lengths of stays were lessened when an emphasis on treatment of patients in their least restrictive environments became a new standard, discharge planning upon admission was encouraged, and clinical protocols that promoted the use of best practices for effective discharge management were implemented.
4) Mandated OT dropped significantly when union leadership and hospital managers created an "all in" plan that rewarded both staff attendance and increased use of voluntary OT instead of mandating.

The final step was to create a sharing process by providing data during monthly department meetings, quarterly all-staff meetings and hospital reports developed by the Quality Assurance Department.

Regardless of what type of organization you are engaged in, implementing Rule #7 remains at the core of moving forward successfully. Goals need to be defined, plans need to be achievable, and success must be shared.

In Summary:

- Your success definition should come from leadership with engagement from others
- Your organization needs to be able to visualize what success will look like
- Goals must be well-defined and achievable
- Progress toward success must be shared on a regular basis

Rule #8 - Use Key Performance Indicators (KPIs) to Standardize Practice

"When variation occurs in the hospital system of care and if the variation results in higher risk and less efficient operations than the variation needs to be addressed by that organization or the system as a whole"

During my time as Deputy Director for the hospitals, a "System of Care" initiative was developed by key leaders of the six various hospitals and central office under my direction. The leadership team included Chief Executive Officers, Chief Clinical Officers, Nurse Executives, Quality Improvement Directors, Chief Operating Officers, Clinical Directors and central office leaders. This group was asked to develop specific Priority Focused Areas (PFAs) for the "System of Care" where they felt both growth and reduced variation in practices needed to occur.

Each of the PFAs had specific measurable objectives that could be translated into Key Performance Indicators (KPIs). The PFAs included the following general areas:

Safety (Risk Reduction), Access (Bed Management), Quality (Standards of Care), Patient Health/Wellness (Clinical Initiative), Recovery (Model of Care Environments), Cost Effective (Resource Management), and Partnerships (Stakeholder Relationships).

Through system discussions and consensus building with the leadership team, three of the PFAs became the structure of a Strategic Plan for the hospitals. Each of the PFAs had teams that developed work plans to address the desired outcomes. Each hospital had representation in each PFA group, and the CEOs were split with two leading each of the work teams. The PFAs and KPIs were as follows:

1) PFA - Improve inpatient access to our hospitals
    a. KPI – Reduce average length of stay (LOS) for newly admitted patients by 10%.

b. KPI - Decrease Readmission rates of discharged patients to less than 3%.
c. KPI – Reduce long term civil and forensic inpatient populations by 10%.

2) PFA - Improve Quality of Care in our hospitals
   a. KPI – Reduce variation in the implementation of three new clinical policies, protocols and guidelines through standardization
   b. KPI – Reduce variation and improve reviewing body scores through system wide performance improvement by providing one system training on the adoption of a culture that promotes and supports critical thinking and a standardized performance improvement model in the hospitals.
   c. KPI – Increase sharing and learning related to survey standard readiness, findings, and responsiveness through the implementation of transparent communication processes that supports monthly meeting of QA Directors.

3) PFA - Improve Patient Safety in our Hospitals
   a. KPI – Reduce occurrences of suicide/self-harm events by 15% through the implementation of enhanced clinical practices and facility modifications in the built environments.
   b. KPI – Reduce episodes of restraint and patient/staff injuries by 15%.
   c. KPI – Assure safety in medication management by eliminating inefficient non automated processes in areas of medication procurement through the purchase of new automated medication machines on all units.

I found that since variation of practice had been a historical issue in hospitals, the use of the above process had several positive outcomes.

As the hospital leaders began working together, a consensus on what was important for hospitals to concentrate on became evident and shared vision and goals were now accepted by leadership.

Even though this is a psychiatric hospital system example, I believe any organization that has multiple sites, and multiple leaders would benefit from being engaged in Rule #8 and employing the PFA/KPI process as it brings focus to an organization and the leadership team.

In Summary:

- In large organizations one set of KPIs is essential
- Your KPIs need to be based on performance measures related to you goals and vision
- Sharing your progress related to your KPI scores is necessary to demonstrate success

Rule #9 – Data Doesn't Lie

"What does the data tell you about moving the needle?"

I really enjoy data. I get excited when I can see charts, spreadsheets, or data bases that tell a story of something that I am interested in. This goes back to my days in grad school when we began using computers to organize our work and create something new.

During the various projects that I have been responsible for over the years, I was regularly questioned about the amount of progress we were making by leadership. What I eventually found was that if I have data, the discussion can be moved from issues with the project itself to the data that I was collecting.

I have previously shared that I always needed a clearly defined vision when I wanted to move a project forward. (Rule #6). The next step would then be the development of a plan (Rule #7) followed by performance indicators (Rule #8) or data.

Data becomes important throughout a project, not just at the finish line. I have found that the best way to show progress during the implementation of a plan is through the use of a data instrument. The use of various types of charts that will show movement or progress over time is essential. Data should be shared with leadership related to how progress is being made, or not, regardless of what has occurred.

I have also found that by using time elements in line and control charts, I can show the progress of the project and where certain activities, or key landmarks, are being met. Therefore, the sharing of data allows me to show the level of movement that is occurring at certain points in time. In addition, through the use of charts and data sets, decisions related to changes in a project can be tracked to see whether progress is being made, or the needle is being moved in a positive direction.

As I continued in my leadership role with the hospital system, my staff would come to me concerned about the progress of their projects or a new plan. My first questions would most likely be what do you think is going on? Can you provide me a story on what you think is happening? And finally, "Show me your data and tell me what you see because data doesn't lie."

In Summary:

- Discussions related to performance should always include data
- Without data you have nothing to show your staff and customers
- Data should be shared with the organization through the use of charts and other tools

Rule # 10 – Lead with the Right Temperament

"When shown a respectful calmness, staff will embrace your leadership."

I have witnessed a few leaders who felt that they needed to demonstrate a certain level of power when directing their organization. These leaders had a reputation of appearing mean-spirited and very demeaning to their staff, not only when bad outcomes occurred but also in general when addressing subordinates. I had difficulty grasping the reason for these behaviors, except that these leaders acted that way to possibly overcome their own inadequacies. When I interacted with them, I found that they did not see respect as an important value, but rather a sign of weakness.

I believe that if an individual consistently behaves in a disrespectful way, they lose their effectiveness when strong leadership is actually called upon and appropriate. I view this type of leadership style as unhealthy to an organization that needs to focus on providing goal-driven health care to their patients, let alone supporting staff that arrive every day to provide the best patient care. During my time as a leader in various systems, I tried to carry myself with a temperament that valued my employees, was interested in their contributions to the organization, and expected them to return the same respectful manners to me as I did to them.

In trying to define my own temperament, I think I could best be described as seeking to being attentive to my staff, especially my leaders. I have found that listening closely to everyone without becoming judgmental or being critical of their thoughts, and ideas, could seem difficult to some, but without remaining open, I believe I may miss an opportunity to learn or even do some teaching.

I have tried to appear calm regardless of the situation. I generally never saw value in making fun of someone or downgrading opinions that I found unacceptable. Most often, my response tended to be something like "I never thought of that before" or "that might work in the right situation." My belief is that by displaying a respectful temperament, the staff I worked with were more receptive to my feedback and behaved likewise. I also, however, have had situations where a strong calm response was not only necessary but required, especially in an emergency.

I have had my own issues with certain individuals who were disrespectful to me, and I would try most of the time to not let them know they had pushed my buttons by remaining calm. These interactions were challenging and required a certain internal strength that was difficult to maintain.

I think that by demonstrating a respectful temperament, staff were drawn to me occasionally. It probably didn't hurt that I had so many years of experience in the system and very rarely could be surprised by something that happened. Toward the end of my career, I found that leaders from all over the system would call upon me to provide thoughts and opinions. I felt that they appreciated my insight because I didn't get excited and kept a calm temperament when helping staff put out their individual fires.

In Summary:

- Staff need to feel valued and respected at all times
- When leaders are disrespectful, they demonstrate a weak style of management
- If staff are the recipients of respectful communication, they will be responsive and support your leadership.

Chapter 3: Rules for Management / Successful Change Management

Rule # 11 – Connect to the Why

"The why' makes change understandable. Without it, no one cares."

When I was in a leadership role overseeing the change from a hybrid health record system to an electronic one, the first thing the vendor impressed on our team was the need to share "the why" to everyone who will be our customer/staff. They shared with our team that anyone using the new system would be involved in a major change to their existing documentation processes as well as their workflow. The message we were asked to deliver had more to do with assisting staff in finding the value of all of the changes that they were going to go through, or in other words "the why."

When we began sharing our plan to implement this change, we started by reviewing with the clinical leadership team and working with them to identify areas of value in this new workflow. These areas were then listed in a series of "why" statements, such as:

1) Standard documentation based on best practices
2) Standard documentation processes that reduce errors
3) Standard documentation that improves patient safety
4) Standard documentation that meets reviewing bodies standards of care
5) Standard documentation processes that create efficiencies
6) Standard documentation processes that will increase system revenue

The next step that we embarked on was sharing all of the "why" statements with the staff. Hospital leadership created posters and monthly newsletters that emphasized the reasons for the change. Each of the six hospitals then appointed change champions that included nurses, physicians, clinicians, and hospital leaders. All of these champions were asked to embrace these "why" statements and use them in their work with the staff as we implemented the change.

By using these strategies, my team and I found that the system staff began to demonstrate excitement and enthusiasm toward the project. Staff wanted to be identified as champions and trainers as we moved closer to implementation.

On our "Go Live" date, more than one hundred dedicated staff began a commitment journey to implement our new EHR. I was very pleased to see how this project came to a successful end with the complete installation of the new system for the 1,000 patients and 1,900 staff that began to use it overnight. As we began to measure our success, we returned to our "why" statements because that was where we had been directing our work.

I have been involved in many projects but none as big or important as this one, and clearly, the lesson learned here is worth sharing. When directing change, leaders must make every effort to connect and direct back to the "why" or the "value" of the new process, no matter how painful it might be.

In Summary:

- Staff need to understand the value of the change
- Staff should be included in developing "Why Statements"
- These statements should be communicated to everyone
- Successful change can be measured through the final results if the value is shared

Rule # 12 - Creating an All in Culture

"How do you create a robust communication culture that staff can buy into?"

In my experience communication gaps are prevalent in organizations that don't pay attention to what is going on and who is saying what. It is difficult to maintain a message to everyone you interact with if you don't have a plan or process on how you are going to do it. In many situations, leaders need to provide guidance to their team related to how they want the organization's work to be perceived.

I believe that it is imperative that leadership articulate not only who they are but who they want to be. This helps staff identify how they fit within the system culture. This is an important issue when you want to change something or move the organization in a different direction. Therefore, in order to create this "All in Culture", especially during organization changes, leaders must develop relationships and communicate the necessity of everyone being all in.

I worked for over fifteen years as the COO of a hospital with a very dynamic CEO. This individual was always on the move and probably could have taught the Management by Walking Around (MBWA) style of leadership. He would leave his office all the time, and we often had to send out the troops to locate him when he was late for meetings or needed to take a call. It was during these trips out of the office that he would visit staff from all disciplines and engage in conversations about why they worked at the hospital and what could be improved related to taking care of patients.

Staff appreciated him because he showed a genuine interest in them as a person and an employee. He consistently conveyed a message to staff on his walks that our goals were to take good care of patients and take care of each other. He always made himself available and tried to address any issues that were brought to him related to fixing problems.

He consistently provided a message that every employee was able to understand; that what we did was important to our patients and their families, and we needed to be "all in" on how we worked together. He not only shared this message with staff but also with the stakeholders of the hospital, including system leadership, agencies we interacted with, and the families of the patients we served.

Because of his charismatic leadership style, my job when I followed him as the next CEO became a bit of a challenge. I began by developing a goal to maintain the same "All in Culture" that my predecessor had demonstrated. I started by operating in a similar management style while simultaneously developing a new culture that was built on where we had come from. As I mentioned in Rule #6, this began by sharing my vision of respect and infusing it as a key component of our work culture. In addition, I also used a lesson-learned leadership approach to help us define how to support staff while demonstrating a respectful model of care as the major theme for our hospital.

The most important step I took was creating an open communication process for all staff and patients using respect as the key. Since respect was not a difficult concept, we soon found that we had developed an "All in Culture" that was based on that theme. As I implemented my own MBWA habits and processes, staff embraced not only my leadership style but my message.

In Summary:

- Having a shared vision and values is a key to developing a partnership with all staff
- Open communication is the key to staff buying into the organizations culture
- Relationships within all levels will move you closer to everyone being "All In"

Rule #13 - Embrace and Become Comfortable with Adversity

"Change may create adversity that will lead to growth in your organization if managed well"

Adversity sometimes is brought on due to both external and internal circumstances such as new leadership, budget problems, or an event that becomes a crisis. Regardless of the type of adversity, these situations can create tension in any organization. Eventually, this may lead to significant changes and conflicts as the problems are being resolved. Good managers should not shy away from embracing change during these times but rather view them as necessary for the growth of the organization.

As a young manager, I tended to withdraw from the internal tension that arose during times of change. I spent more energy focusing on how the change would negatively impact my work and the goals of my team rather than how growth was possible in the long run. It wasn't until I managed my team through several of these events that I came to the realization that not only are these situations necessary at times for growth, but they also may be rewarding.

As I started to understand the need for change and to embrace conflict, I began looking forward to new processes or programs. I eventually started to create some communication structures in my work area that allowed my team to discuss their feelings about change. The first approach I used was to assist staff in recognizing their discomfort with a change. I used the following questions to help staff deal with their feelings of conflict and the tension that came with it:

1) Do you understand the change, why it is necessary, and do you see value in the change?
2) Can you share what type of conflict you are going to experience due to the change?

3) How do you see the change affecting your work?
4) How do you see the change affecting you personally?
5) What can we do to support you during the change?

I would eventually share my own experience with change, how conflict is created, and how it leads to better outcomes if you embrace it. I would also model my own responses to previous situations and how I grew, and the organization grew from it.

I believe it is natural for staff and managers to express concern about change, adversity, and conflict. Indeed, there is always a tendency to find fault with anything that is not the "same way we did it before" or "not the way we always operated". Managers need to recognize these tendencies in their staff and address them in order to move the team forward. I think that letting staff express their issues or concerns is certainly acceptable, but it should not be encouraged beyond letting it out and then moving on.

In Summary:

- Adversity is necessary sometimes in order for organizations to grow and improve
- Do not shy away from the tension that comes with change but find ways to address it with staff
- Learning how to accept adversity is a step toward your organization's maturity

Rule #14 - Keep Progress Moving / Don't Quit

"Many times, failure leads to success if you don't give up."

It took me 10 years to succeed with one of my special projects. I unfortunately failed twice before I was finally able to get to the finish line. I believe that most individuals would have quit or been fired, but I never allowed that to happen because I always had a new plan in the works.

My first attempt was based on an understanding with another organization that they could produce a product that could meet our needs at a specific cost. Our staff worked closely with this organization, and it looked promising. But when they kept raising the price and eventually it went to an unacceptable level, we had to walk away and move on.

The second attempt was well planned out, and we committed many resources to assure success. The cost was acceptable, and the vendor promised to provide a product that could meet our needs. Then, one third of the way through implementation, it became clear to our team and the hospitals involved that the product did not provide what was promised, and we had to walk away again.

The third attempt hit the target. Our team learned from the previous failures, and we created a plan that would assure success. We started with using information related to best practices and resource management for this type of project. We received a commitment to fund it. Then we developed a project description in cooperation with our staff and the hospital staff, many of whom would go on to be the main users of it. We ended up with more than five hundred specific recommendations. Thus, we made the project acceptance contingent on vendors meeting these standards in order to be considered. The top vendors that bid on it each did demonstrations for our team and leadership staff, who then had a voice in our choice. Today the project has been viewed as an overwhelming success, and our team has received accolades from others, including some state agencies, on our process for assuring a great outcome.

When I am asked what my biggest accomplishments are, I point to this project but clarify that I had to fail twice before we could get it done. If I would have quit or allowed someone to step in and tell me to stop, then this would never have happened. But we did not let that get in the way. The leadership team that we worked with had confidence in our implementation team because we demonstrated that we could and would get it done and provided them a path to accomplish our task.

The support of our leaders and staff were the key in getting this done. During this journey we had multiple issues and support was difficult at times. I can take some credit for not giving up and being persistent. I could have walked away at any time, but when you have a dream along with an attitude that you are going to achieve something never done before and not fail again, success is not only possible, it is assured.

In Summary:

- Learn from previous failures and use that to create success
- Maintain engagement with your leadership team and demonstrate competence
- If your finish line is a dream that you can share, your staff will become followers.

Chapter 4: Rules for Promoting Respect

Rule #15 - Develop Relationships with Your Friends and Enemies

"Addressing issues is more effective if relationships have already been established with all parties involved"

When I was appointed CEO of the hospital, I started quarterly meetings with all the agencies that we interacted with. The attendees of these meetings included me as well as our Medical Director, Nursing Director, Clinical Services Director, and Chief Operating Officer. The agencies would bring leaders who were responsible for managing their system and had a history of working with us. We would alternate meeting in person on and off site to go over any changes in our systems, review our perceptions of how we were working together, and provide performance data.

Early on, we spent a significant amount of time sharing our hospital's new Respect Initiative and how we expected to work with each agency as a stakeholder with a respectful tone and attitude. We then moved on to performance data related to the agencies' operations, including use of hospital beds, lengths of stay for specific populations, and any issues that the data could illustrate. During these meetings, a major topic always surfaced related to the management of difficult patients and the resources needed to manage those individuals in the community.

Between our group and our agency partners, we each took turns giving an update on staffing matters and sharing issues related to shortages that could have impacted efficient patient care. I found that during these sharing sessions, there was a higher level of camaraderie among all those involved, as we began to appreciate and become more aware of each other's hurdles.

More than just the exchange of data, the real benefit of these quarterly meetings was effective problem solving. As we and our partners began to work closer together, we built relationships through our in-person meetings, and communication during crises rarely became a problem. If we had issues, there was a level of commitment to work it out and not personalize problems if a disagreement occurred.

I did find, however, that if our leadership group, especially me, did not already have a good relationship built with the leaders from another agency, then communication would sometimes become strained and addressing issues more difficult. I never felt that I had to like people to work with them, but I did find that if I had spent some time with them and had established a level of respectful communication beforehand, problems became easier to solve.

On the other hand, I did run into a few stakeholders who were, maybe not enemies, but so negative that respectful communication became a chore. In those cases, I discovered that by reminding them that our mission and purpose was to take care of patients the best we could and to do it in a respectful way, their tone would change a bit. I was not always successful but before I gave up, I wanted to try to move the conversation in a different direction. In addition, working on these relationships became a future strategic goal for our team.

In Summary:

- Having previous respectful communication with others is a key to addressing difficult situations when they occur
- Good relationships will lead to commitment when faced with areas of concern
- Without a desire on both sides to view an issue respectfully attention to each other's basic responsibilities as an organization should be emphasized.

Rule # 16 - Feeling Safe is a Must

"It is hard for staff and patients to engage in recovery if they don't feel safe and respected"

During the time when our hospital implemented the Respect Initiative (Rule #6), we were challenged by a work environment that included patients who, at times, could be violent and create tension in the inpatient psychiatric unit's therapeutic milieu. Even more problematic, however, was when we tried to introduce a Recovery Treatment model into that environment.

The Recovery model has historically been a tool utilized in substance abuse treatment that emphasizes supporting an individual's personal strengths. It encourages the care provider to support the person in the development of a path away from addiction and on to mental wellness.

During our work to introduce the Recovery model, we first began by engaging the clinical staff who we believed could help us identify how to utilize both the Respect Initiative and our Recovery Model together while reducing violence on our units. What we found was that the combination of recovery and respect blended well together and contributed to a good outcome for the staff and patients.

As described previously, when we implemented the Respect Initiative into our therapeutic milieu, both patients and staff were asked to find ways to be respectful toward each other. For the employees, this meant adopting new behaviors such as recognizing patients as people first and not by a diagnosis or a legal status. More emphasis was placed on listening to our patients and treating everyone, not just our patients but also the staff in a way that they would like to be treated. Recovery focused care plans began to replace old-fashioned problem-oriented treatment plans, then comfort and safety plans were developed and designed with the individual patient as well as their clinical team to reduce aggression.

Probably the strongest component of the adoption and implementation process was the emphasis on developing a therapeutic relationship between our clinical staff and the patients themselves. When we did so, it became easier for the staff to engage with these patients when stressing that they are people first. In addition, staff were trained in how to incorporate respectful language and behaviors into the community meetings and therapy groups on the units.

The issue of patient aggression was more difficult to manage, but we saw remarkable results when patients were given the opportunity to share with staff how frustrated they became when they were not listened to and when they felt disrespected. In response, we eliminated hands-on procedures and replaced them with clinical time outs for patients who just needed to find a place on the unit to feel safe. We also added comfort rooms that could be used instead of seclusion or restraint rooms and added comfort items, such as snacks and other items patients had identified as something they could relate to.

As this work progressed, staff and patients soon began to share with leadership how safer their units had become. In addition, we found through our data collection, that if people were treated with respect and with an emphasis on recovery, they will have a better chance to leave the hospital and remain in the community longer without episodes of violence.

In Summary:

- Recovery is a clinical process that recognizes individual personal strengths and embraces people first language
- Being respectful is a component of the recovery model
- When staff and patients view respect and recovery as a healthy model of care a safe environment will follow

Rule # 17 – Become Coercion Free

"Minimize power struggles in your treatment culture"

As the CEO in the hospital, I worked with my team to seek out ways to reduce restraint usage also described in rule #16. The use of restraints not only conflicted with our use of the Recovery Treatment model but also was inconsistent with the use of respect as a major focus of our hospital culture. In addition, research had shown that the utilization of restraint and seclusion interventions are the most unsafe processes in a hospital, and most staff and patient injuries occur during the process of restraining patients.

In our hospital, we started looking at data and attempted to identify the root causes of this high-risk process. We began by sharing a new organizational goal of reducing its usage, minimizing injuries, and creating a safer hospital. Our team developed a review process for each restraint incident with an emphasis on identifying the "why" it was occurring. A list of causes was developed and shared with leadership.

It soon became clear to our team that we had multiple issues, but many events were occurring due to some type of interaction between patients and staff. Unit rules that the staff had put in place began to surface as a problem. Simple things like when the patients could get their coffee, when they could take a shower, and when they could go to bed were brought forward. We found that these things may have sounded harmless but if not implemented fairly could and did cause unnecessary conflicts leading to bad outcomes.

We appointed the hospital safety officer as the point person to investigate each episode of restraint and interview everyone engaged in the event. If staff or patients were injured, he would perform a deep dive into the process that was used during the restraint process and whether staff were using the hospital's approved procedures. Immediately following the restraint, the CEO was called to make them aware of the situation. Each of these events were also discussed during the morning nursing report that was attended by all leadership staff. Eventually the Quality Assurance Director was asked to provide an overview of what happened and provide recommendations to our staff, especially with regard to what type of staff-to-patient interaction may have led to the restraint.

We created a subcommittee of the hospital's restraint and seclusion reduction committee and labeled it the coercion free team in an effort to address our concerns. They began defining the unfavorable coercion activities that were present in the hospital milieu, especially those that were not supported by hospital policy. For example, the hospital did not have a policy that dictated coffee distribution times, shower times, or bedtimes. The hospital did, however, have policies that patients should have a voice in their care. Therefore, it was decided that rules should be based on the understanding that the residential unit was a community that needed to demonstrate respect to everyone, and unnecessary rules should be eliminated. Staff were then challenged to find respectful ways to interact with patients and even encouraged to eliminate the use of the word "no" on their units.

New training programs were developed that included descriptions of bad outcomes and provided new options for staff to use as an intervention when a patient was in crisis. Videos were created demonstrating these new staff behaviors that involved the use of respectful language and new de-escalation skills. Our new coercion free team created a logo, called "Work Safe/Work Smart," and provided monthly reports to each unit related to their use of restraints. As major reductions occurred, these changes were celebrated by leadership with special recognition to units that made the best progress toward restraint reduction.

Within one year, restraint usage and injuries to patients and staff were reduced significantly. Our team eventually wrote up our program and it was selected to be published as "Best Practices: Safety Guidelines for

Injury Free Management of Psychiatric Inpatients in Pre-Crisis and Crisis Situations," which was published in the December 2008 edition of *Psychiatric Services*.

Although this entire process started as a challenge to reduce bad outcomes in the hospital, it turned into an outstanding piece of work by our team. It was accomplished by placing an emphasis on our goals, our use of the Respect Initiative, and encouraging critical team members to step up and move the needle. We became a safer, less coercive hospital with staff who were more confident in managing a high-risk process.

In Summary:

- Power struggles in a treatment environment are not healthy and at times appear disrespectful
- The overuse of rules and not listening to patients creates conflicts that lead to unsafe situations
- The elimination of any unnecessary rules moves toward coercion free care space

Rule # 18 – Promote Peer Support Programs

"Listen to your peers and they will find better ways for you to provide care"

My hospital became one of the first in the State of Ohio to launch a peer support program. This initiative allowed former patients who had previously been admitted to our hospital and had successfully lived in the community for at least five years to return as employees. These individuals also had to demonstrate they were actively participating in their outpatient programming including their medication compliance and substance abuse support programs if required by their case manager. The key service the peer supporters provided can be located in their title, "support." At times our staff would rely on these individuals to communicate with a patient who was having issues with finding themselves in a psychiatric hospital.

The peers would work a maximum of 20 hours a week for a couple years and then move to full-time employment after receiving evaluations that described their competence in this role. They had several defined duties including: 1) meeting and orienting new admissions to the hospital and answering questions, 2) attending community meetings and offering time to meet with any patient who may feel they need additional support, and 3) attending treatment teams when asked by a patient to advocate for them.

Many of the peer supporters who worked in our hospital were key contributors to patient care and were invaluable to our patients improving in their personal recovery. Although I could provide a multitude of examples of our peers' work, I would like to highlight one specific individual whose efforts exemplify the value of these individuals to our system. His name was Joe for this rule, and he was severely mentally ill at a young age. Tragically, he killed his parents because, as he describes it, "the voices were telling him to do it." When he arrived at our hospital, he was not aware that he was mentally ill.

He told us that he thought everyone heard voices and it was normal for that to happen. It wasn't until he started taking medications and learning about mental illness that he understood what happened. His guilt was tremendous and not only did he have to deal with that but also the overwhelming negative feelings from his family.

Joe had to get permission from the court during his treatment to move through the hospital's internal movement level system. He first moved from maximum security to minimum security including movement on hospital grounds with supervision, to movement without supervision and finally discharge. It took over ten years for Joe to demonstrate to his psychiatrist and his treatment team and the courts that he had accepted his illness and would remain compliant with on-going treatment in the community, a treatment that required very close supervision for an extended period of time.

Even though he had committed a horrendous crime while ill, Joe was well-liked in the hospital and was looked upon by staff as an ideal patient. Several years after discharge he applied and was accepted into the hospital peer support program and was called upon to assist staff with the management of some very difficult cases.

His story is one of hope and resilience, and he was able to share it with patients. He could testify to everyone how, just because you have an illness, it doesn't mean your life is over. He refers to his time at the hospital as lifesaving and was a great example to not only the patients but the staff, that people can recover and live a full life.

During my tenure as CEO, I called upon Joe to speak to our hospital staff during small respect group meetings. He would talk about his story, but he would also share how he felt as a patient in the hospital and how at times he was disrespected. The staff in attendance would ask for feedback from him on how they could have demonstrated respect for him and other patients. These group meetings became growth opportunities for everyone, and the overall response from staff indicated they now found they could do a better job since they understood how the patients felt.

Over time, Joe and the other peer supporters gained confidence from the respect that they felt from leadership and the clinical staff, and they began to influence institutional policy as they became members of every hospital committee. Indeed, the peers created a video presentation that was titled "Making a Difference with Hope and Respect," and the hospital started using it during respect small group sessions. Eventually it was added to the employee orientation program and also was shared in the lobby of the hospital.

I believe that Joe and the other peers demonstrate the value of sharing how the work we do as health care workers has an impact on someone's life. We may find it difficult at times to see that it is possible in health care to make a difference, but if we as leaders value what we hear and incorporate the feedback in how we manage our care, the change will be very rewarding.

Thanks to Joe and the other peers.

Note: When I became Deputy Director of the hospital system, I made Peer Support programs mandatory in all of the hospitals.

In Summary:

- When peers share their experience, everyone learns more
- Peer supporters are key contributors to patient care and a valuable reinforcer to the recovery model of care
- The success demonstrated by peer support programs reinforces to staff and patients that mental illness is not the end of their life journey,

Key Points

Chapter 1: Rules for Supervisors / Successful Managers

Rule # 1 - Tell people what you want them to do

"Tell people what you want them to do because if you don't, they will make it up and it probably is not what you want them to do".

- Have regularly scheduled meetings in person with staff
- Share with staff and confirm with them what you see as their job
- Set Expectations in a clear manner
- Provide support and guidance on what success look like
- Review it during your meetings and share how it fits in the goals of the organization.

Rule # 2 – Staff Don't Want to Mess Up

"I don't believe that people get up in the morning and decide they are going to mess up at work that day."

- People want to be successful at their jobs.
- People want to feel respected and recognized for their work performance
- People do not intentionally make unacceptable decisions
- Managers must do more than provide information to employees and expect improvement
- Managers need to build a culture of respect
- If given the opportunity and motivation, people will choose to excel.

Rule #3 - Don't Bring a Problem Forward without Bringing a Solution
"If I am solving my staff's problems for them then I am doing their job and not supporting their growth."

- Staff can solve their own problems
- By defining and owning a problem staff can create solutions
- Coming to their manager with solutions will assist staff in the development of their critical thinking skills

Rule #4 - Don't Negotiate with Terrorists
"Responding to demands by employees should never be rewarded"

- How you respond to your staff will create issues in your organization if not managed well
- "My way or the highway" and staff threats are unacceptable behaviors
- Respectful interactions as a leader will support a culture that promotes respect
- If you Interact and give in to employees who value themselves above the organization and their fellow staff, then you lessen the value of that person.

Chapter 2: Rules for Leaders / Successful Leadership

Rule #5 – Get to the Yes
"Can you get me to a yes on this?"
- Define broadly what the "yes" could look like
- Shape a solution that could be redefined by the audience, but manage it yourself
- By communicating respectfully, acceptance of your plan is predictable

Rule #6 – Use Your Vision to Provide Leadership and Develop Leaders
"The best process that I found when I wanted to move an organization or a group of staff toward a specific goal was to use a process that utilized a vision".
- Your vision statement should be clear and easy to understand
- Start with goal language that staff can relate to and includes "follow me and come this way"
- Involve and support a team of leaders that will be empowered to get it to the finish line.

Rule #7 – Define Success and Share It
"As leaders, we need to be able to define what success looks like to your organization so your staff can appreciate their efforts and know where they fit as they attempt to achieve success"
- Your success definition should come from leadership with engagement from others
- Your organization needs to be able to visualize what success will look like
- Goals must be well-defined and achievable
- Progress toward success must be shared on a regular basis

Rule #8 - Use Key Performance Indicators (KPIs) to Standardize Practice

"When variation occurs in the hospital system of care and if the variation results in higher risk and less efficient operations than the variation needs to be addressed by that organization or the system as a whole"

- In large organizations one set of KPIs is essential
- Your KPIs need to be based on performance measures related to you goals and vision
- Sharing your progress related to your KPI scores is necessary to demonstrate success

Rule #9 – Data Doesn't Lie

"What does the data tell you about moving the needle?"

- Discussions related to performance should always include data
- Without data you have nothing to show your staff and customers
- Data should be shared with the organization through the use of charts and other tools

Rule # 10 – Lead with the Right Temperament

"By showing a respectful calmness, staff will embrace your leadership"

- Staff need to feel valued and respected at all times
- When leaders are disrespectful, they demonstrate a weak style of management
- If staff are the recipients of respectful communication, they will be responsive and support your leadership.

Chapter 3: Rules for Management / Successful Change Management

Rule # 11 – Connect to the Why
"The why makes change understandable, without it no one cares"
- Staff need to feel valued and respected at all times
- When leaders are disrespectful, they demonstrate a weak style of management
- If staff are the recipients of respectful communication, they will be responsive and support your leadership.

Rule # 12 - Creating an All in Culture
"How do you create a robust communication culture that staff can buy into?"
- Having a shared vision and values is a key to developing a partnership with all staff
- Open communication is the key to staff buying into the organizations culture
- Relationships within all levels will move you closer to everyone being "All In"

Rule #13 - Embrace and Become Comfortable with Adversity
"Change may create adversity that will lead to growth in your organization if managed well"
- Adversity is necessary sometimes in order for organizations to grow and improve
- Do not shy away from the tension that comes with change but find ways to address it with staff
- Learning how to accept adversity is a step toward your organization's maturity

Rule #14 - Keep Progress Moving / Don't Quit
"Many times, failure leads to success if you don't give up"
- Learn from previous failures and use that to create success
- Maintain engagement with your leadership team and demonstrate competence
- If your finish line is a dream that you can share, your staff will become followers.

Chapter 4: Rules for Promoting Respect

Rule #15 - Develop Relationships with Your Friends and Enemies
"Addressing issues is more effective if relationships have already been established with all parties involved"
- Having previous respectful communication with others is a key to addressing difficult situations when they occur
- Good relationships will lead to commitment when faced with areas of concern
- Without a desire on both sides to view an issue respectfully attention to each other's basic responsibilities as an organization should be emphasized.

Rule # 16 - Feeling Safe is a Must
" It is hard for staff and patients to engage in recovery if they don't feel safe and respected"
- Recovery is a clinical process that recognizes individual personal strengths and embraces people first language.
- Being respectful is a component of the recovery model
- When staff and patients view respect and recovery as a healthy model of care a safe environment will follow

Rule # 17 – Become Coercion Free
"Minimize power struggles in your treatment culture"
- Power struggles in a treatment environment are not healthy and at times appear disrespectful
- The overuse of rules and not listening to patients creates conflicts that lead to unsafe situations
- The elimination of any unnecessary rules moves toward coercion free care space

Rule # 18 – Promote Peer Support Programs

"Listen to your peers and they will find better ways for you to provide care"

- When peers share their experience, everyone learns more
- Peer supporters are key contributors to patient care and a valuable reinforcer to the recovery model of care
- The success demonstrated by peer support programs reinforces to staff and patients that mental illness is not the end of their life journey,

Conclusion / Acknowledgements

The idea of publishing "Bob's Rules" was really encouraged by my team of staff at the department. Many times, I would share my rules based on something that had occurred previously and later became a success story of some kind. Folks would pass these along and reference me as someone who had led some successful projects but always had a great team to support him.

Some of these rules that you have probably already found are rather simple such as "Tell People What You Want Them to Do" or "Don't Bring a Problem Without Bringing a Solution."." But I have found that sometimes a simple way of operating provides a structure that is easy for everyone to use and replicate.

The more complicated rules dealt with the difficulties that leaders face when they are involved in projects that may challenge them such as "Get to the Yes" and "Define Success and Share It." I also felt I needed to reference performance data as a key to assuring success as well.

I enjoyed passing on my rules related to change management including "Connect to the Why" and "Keep Progress Moving/Don't Quit." This is probably the situation that requires the most significant thoughtful communication from leaders in order for your team to visualize where you want them to go.

Finally, sharing my absolutely favorite topic of "Respect" was the appropriate ending to this publication to me. "Feeling Safe is a Must" was a struggle to make happen as well as how to "Become Coercion Free" but without my team working on the hospital's Respect Initiative it wouldn't have been possible. Sharing Joe's story in "Promote a Strong Peer Support Program" was the best way that I feel I could come up with to finish my rules about respectful leadership.

My hope for those who have taken the time to read this publication is for you to find some new ways to work with your leadership team and your staff. My goal for you is that you feel empowered to move your organization with a new attitude that promotes communication and respectful values.

With Respect,

Bob

About the Author

Bob Short was born and raised on the east side of Detroit where he attended Catholic Grade School and High School. He received his bachelor's degree in occupational therapy from Eastern Michigan University and his master's degree in public administration from the Ohio State University.

Bob spent over 45 years working in the Ohio Department of Mental Health in various leadership roles as a COO and CEO of a hospital and Deputy Director of Hospital Services. He has authored several professional articles related to the subjects of safe hospital process, peer support programs and dual diagnosis treatment.

He and his wife live presently in Grandview Heights Ohio, a suburb of Columbus, where they spend a significant amount of time with their four married children and eight grandchildren, who all live close by.

This is Bob's first book. He has already begun sharing his rules with both private sector and public sector leadership teams since its publication.

Email: RAShort.respect@gmail.com

Ohio Department of Mental Health and Addiction Services Hospital Team 2024

Ribbon Cutting for the new Central Ohio Behavioral Health hospital in Columbus.

www.ingramcontent.com/pod-product-compliance
Lightning Source LLC
LaVergne TN
LVHW021945060526
838200LV00042B/1924